The artwork that appears in this book originally appeared in the picture books *Olivia, Olivia Saves the Circus* and *Olivia…and the Missing Toy* written and illustrated by Ian Falconer and published by Simon & Schuster Children's Publishing.

Licensed by Silver Lining Productions

Quotation on page 64 reprinted from *Oh, the Places You'll Go!* by Dr. Seuss (Theodore Geisel), 1990.

06 07 08 09 10 WKT 10 9 8 7 6 5 4 3 2

ISBN-13: 978-0-7407-5818-8

ISBN-10: 0-7407-5818-7

Library of Congress Control Number: 2005933101

www.andrewsmcmeel.com

DREAM
BIG

starring
OLIVIA™

DREAM BIG

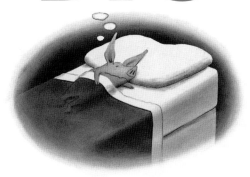

**Andrews McMeel
Publishing®**

Kansas City

Everything starts as somebody's daydream.

—LARRY NIVEN

Logic will get you from A to B.

Imagination will take you anywhere.

—ALBERT EINSTEIN

Sometimes I've believed as many as six

impossible things before breakfast.

—LEWIS CARROLL

It ain't braggin'

if you can back it up.

—DIZZY DEAN

Anything's possible if you've got enough nerve.

—J.K. ROWLING

You can have whatever you want

if you dress for it.

—EDITH HEAD

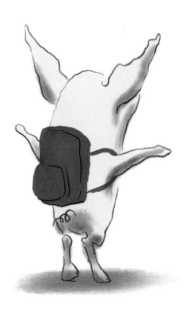

Style...

...is knowing who you are...

—GORE VIDAL

Be who you are and say what you feel,

because those who mind don't matter

and those who matter don't mind.

—Dr. Seuss

Nobody can be exactly like me.

Even I have trouble doing it.

—Tallulah Bankhead

Great spirits
have always
encountered
opposition
from mediocre
minds.

—ALBERT EINSTEIN

I love acting.

It is so much more real than life.

—Oscar Wilde

It's kind of fun to do the impossible.

—WALT DISNEY

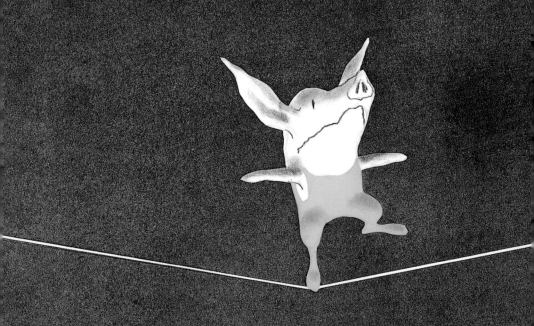

The only people who never **tumble**

are those who never mount the high wire.

—OPRAH WINFREY

A woman is like a tea bag —

you never know how strong she is

until she gets in hot water.

—ELEANOR ROOSEVELT

I don't say we all ought to misbehave,

but we ought to look as if we could.

—ORSON WELLES

If you obey all the rules,

you miss all the fun.

—KATHARINE HEPBURN

Always behave as if nothing had happened,

no matter what has happened.

—Arnold Bennett

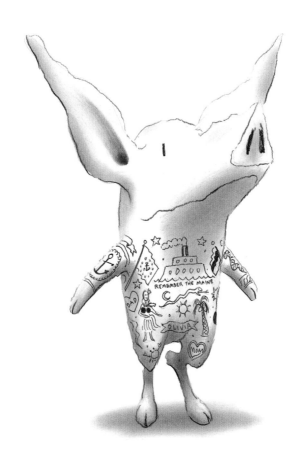

What should I be

but just what I am?

—Edna St. Vincent Millay

Life is short;

live it up.

—Nikita Khrushchev

Life is a ticket

to the greatest show on Earth.

—Martin H. Fischer

If you can't convince them,

confuse them.

—Harry S Truman

Reality leaves a lot to the imagination.

—JOHN LENNON

Dreams say what they mean,

but they don't say it in daytime language.

—GAIL GODWIN

If you don't know

where you are going,

you can never get lost.

—HERB COHEN

Life is something that happens

when you can't get to sleep.

—Fran Lebowitz

Look for the ridiculous in everything

and you will find it.

—Jules Renard

You don't get harmony

when everybody sings the same note.

—DOUG FLOYD

I'm afraid of nothing

except being bored.

—GRETA GARBO

When in doubt...

...wear red.

—BILL BLASS

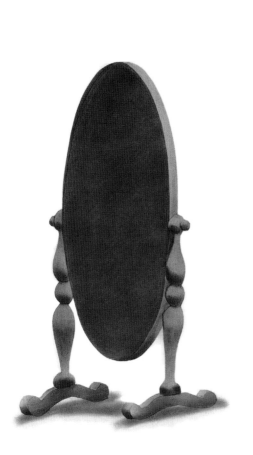

I am just too much.

—BETTE DAVIS

Today is your day!

Your mountain is waiting.

So...*get on your way!*

—DR. SEUSS,
OH, THE PLACES YOU'LL GO!